FAMOUS PLACES MAZES

Journey Through The World!

by Dan Nevins

Watermill Press

Ready for fun?

Here are exciting mazes that will show you the Eiffel Tower...the Great Pyramids...Mount Everest...and other amazing places as you've never seen them before!

So sit back, pick up a pencil, and get ready for an incredible journey of twists and turns.

If you get stuck, answers begin on page 58.

The Alamo

Where in the world is it?
San Antonio, Texas

When the people of Texas decided to become independent from Mexico in 1836, they were attacked by a large Mexican army of 5,000 soldiers. The Texans, who had fewer than 200 men, used the old Spanish mission, the Alamo, as their fort. Fighting against overwhelming odds, the Texans were eventually defeated and all were killed. But their heroic defense gave other Texans enough time to gather their forces, defeat the Mexican Army, and win their independence.

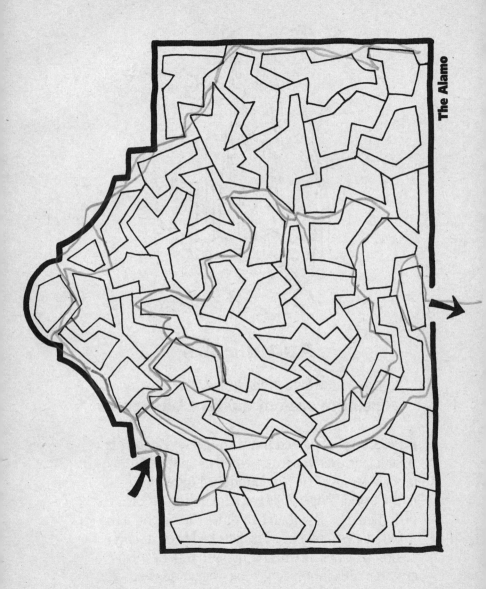

The Alamo

5

Angel Falls

Where in the world is it?
A remote area of eastern Venezuela

In 1935, a pilot named Jimmy Angel was flying his small plane over Venezuela when he spotted an incredible sight. He had found the highest waterfall in the world. Angel Falls has a total drop of 3,212 feet (979 meters), more than two times the height of the world's tallest building. The falls had been discovered before by Native Americans and also by a Spanish explorer. But Jimmy Angel told the world about the falls, and named them after himself.

6

Angel Falls

Big Ben

Where in the world is it?
London, England

Rising above the Houses of Parliament in London is a tall clock tower. Everyone calls the tower Big Ben, but the name is really that of the huge bell inside. A near-perfect timekeeper, Big Ben has tolled the hours since 1859. It was named after Sir Benjamin Hall, a government official at the time the bell was installed.

Big Ben

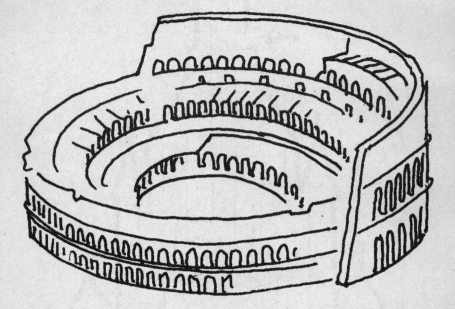

Colosseum

Where in the world is it?
Rome, Italy

Two thousand years ago, in the days of the Roman Empire, huge crowds gathered in the Colosseum to watch gladiator battles and other public spectacles. Up to 50,000 people could fit inside this great outdoor theater. Today, only the ruins of the Colosseum are still standing. But it is still an impressive structure.

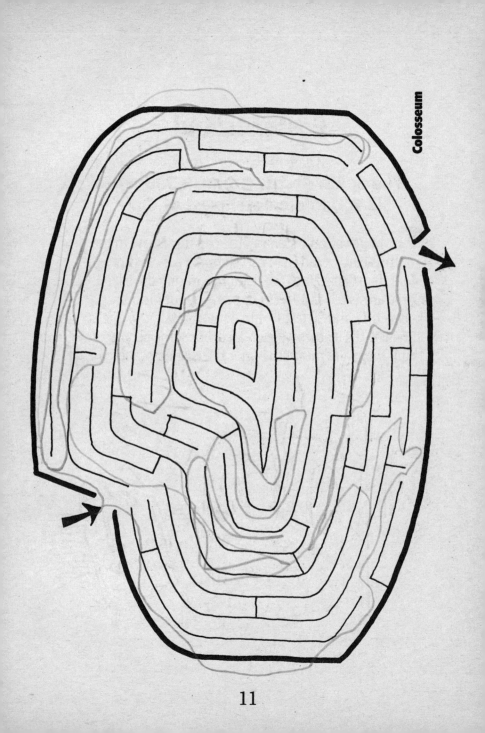

Colosseum

Easter Island

Where in the world is it?
The South Pacific Ocean, 2,300 miles (3,700 kilometers) west of Chile

The huge volcanic stone statues on this island in the South Pacific Ocean were carved hundreds of years ago. More than 600 statues are scattered around the island. Some are as tall as 40 feet (12 meters), but most are between 11 and 20 feet (3.4 to 6 meters) tall. No one is sure why the statues were created, but some people think they were meant to honor the islanders' ancestors.

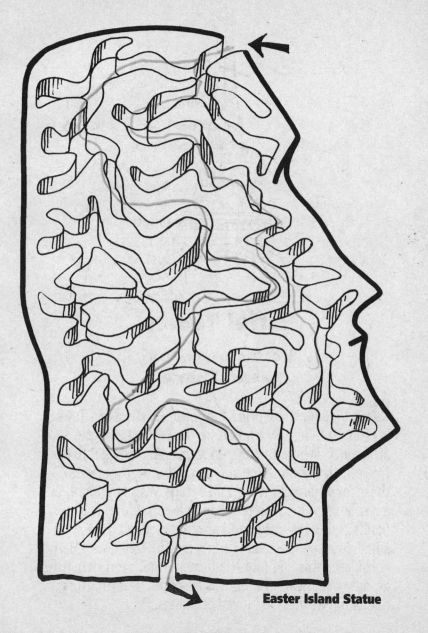

Easter Island Statue

Eiffel Tower

Where in the world is it?
Paris, France

Designed for the World's Fair of 1889, the Eiffel Tower is France's tallest TV transmitter and its biggest tourist attraction. When it first opened, people could get to the top only by climbing the stairs. Of course, there were those for whom climbing 1,710 steps was not enough of a challenge. One man climbed to the first level with his hands tied to his knees, and another reached the top on stilts! Most people today simply use the elevators. Many considered this 984-foot- (300-meter-) tall iron structure an ugly junk heap when it was first built, but now it is one of the world's best-loved buildings.

Eiffel Tower

Empire State Building

Where in the world is it?
New York City

Every year in New York City there is a race in which the runners dash up 102 flights of stairs to the top of the Empire State Building. Of course, King Kong scaled the *outside* of the building to capture actress Fay Wray in the famous 1933 movie. For years, the Empire State Building was the tallest in the world. Although it no longer holds this honor, the views from its observation decks are still among the most spectacular in the world. On a clear day, you can see a 50-mile (80.5-kilometer) panorama from the top of this great building.

Empire State Building

The Great Pyramids

Where in the world are they?
Giza, Egypt

There are many pyramids in Egypt, but the pyramids at Giza are the largest and best-preserved of them all. They were built about 2500 B.C. as a burial place for kings. The largest of the pyramids is made of more than two million stones, each weighing about $2\frac{1}{2}$ tons (2.3 metric tons)!

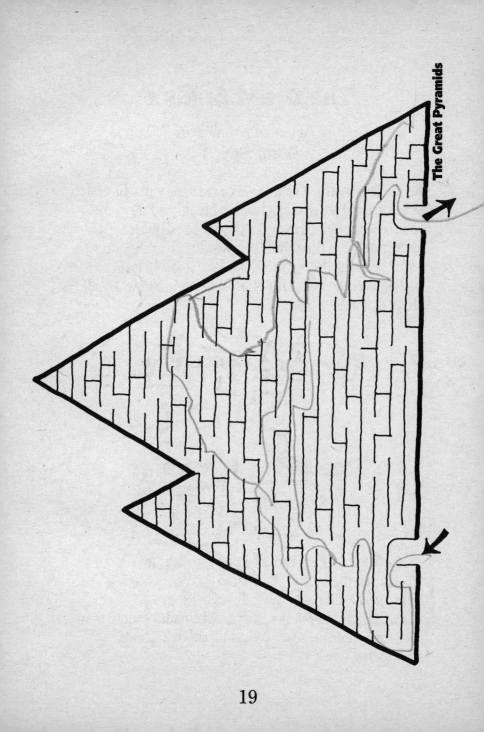

The Great Pyramids

19

The Great Sphinx

Where in the world is it?
Giza, Egypt

In ancient myths, a sphinx was a creature with the body of a lion and the head of a human being. In Egypt, the sphinx became the symbol of the king and queen. The largest statue of the sphinx is called the Great Sphinx, and it lies near the pyramids at Giza. It is 240 feet (73 meters) long and 66 feet (20 meters) high, and was built about 4,500 years ago.

The Great Sphinx

The Great Wall

Where in the world is it?
China

Thousands of years ago, the Chinese were having trouble with invaders on their northern border. So they built a wall to keep their enemies out! The Great Wall of China, built completely by hand, is almost 4,000 miles (6,400 kilometers) long, and 25 feet (7.6 meters) high. The Great Wall is one of the few human-made wonders on Earth visible from the moon.

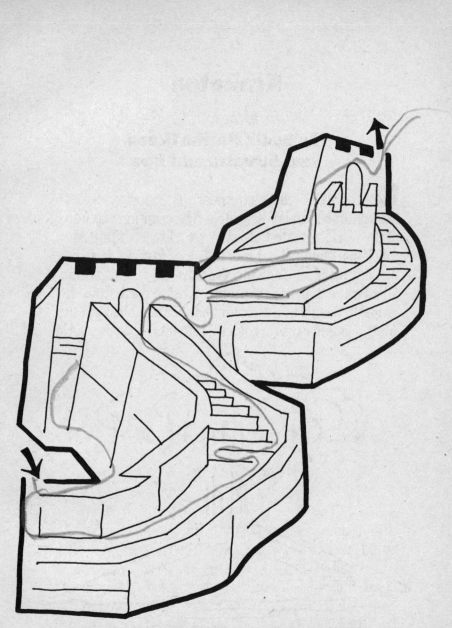

The Great Wall

23

Krakatoa

Where in the world is it?
**The South Pacific Ocean,
near Sumatra and Java**

On August 27, 1883, a tremendous explosion rocked the volcanic island of Krakatoa. The eruption was one of the world's greatest disasters. Rocks were flung 34 miles (54.7 kilometers) into the air! Most of the island was destroyed, and a tidal wave caused by the explosion killed more than 36,000 people. Dust and ash from the eruption floated in the air for about a year, blocking the sun's rays and causing colder weather all over the world.

24

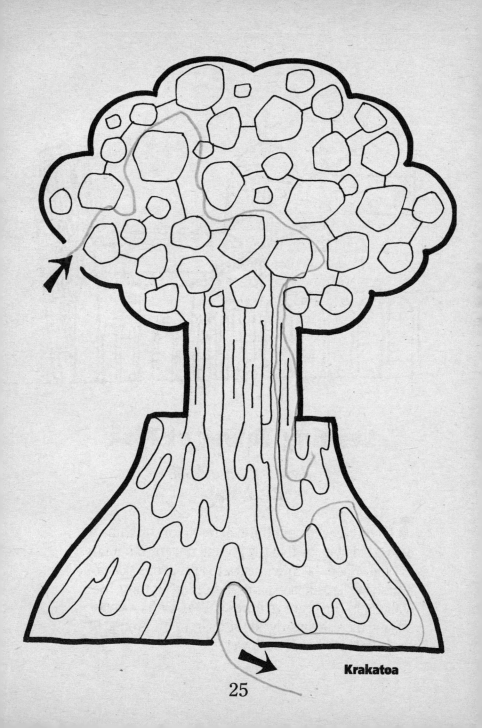

Krakatoa

25

Leaning Tower of Pisa

Where in the world is it?
Pisa, Italy

The people who built this bell tower for the Cathedral of Pisa didn't know that the ground underneath it was too soft. Soon the tower began to lean to one side. But it hasn't fallen. In fact, it's been leaning for more than 600 years! The Leaning Tower is 177 feet (54 meters) tall and there are nearly 300 steps from the ground to the bells at the top of the tower.

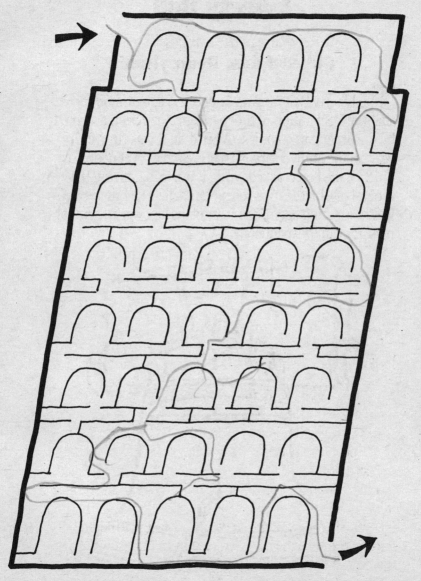

Leaning Tower of Pisa

Liberty Bell

Where in the world is it?
Philadelphia, Pennsylvania

The Liberty Bell rang on July 8, 1776, to announce that the Declaration of Independence had been accepted by the American colonies. After that, it was rung every year on the anniversary of that great day. Then, on July 8, 1835, the bell cracked when it was rung during the funeral of Chief Justice John Marshall. The Liberty Bell was never rung again, but it remains a powerful symbol of American independence.

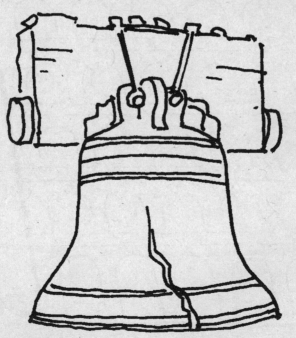

Liberty Bell

Lincoln Memorial

Where in the world is it?
Washington, D.C.

This beautiful monument honors Abraham Lincoln, the 16th president of the United States. It was dedicated in 1922, after seven years of construction. The 36 columns on the outside stand for the 36 states in the Union when Lincoln died. The 19-foot- (5.8-meter-) tall marble statue of Lincoln gazes out toward the Washington Monument. It is one of Washington, D.C.'s most well-known and treasured monuments, and appears on the back of each United States penny and five-dollar bill.

Lincoln Memorial

Little Mermaid

Where in the world is it?
Copenhagen, Denmark

Ships sailing into Copenhagen's harbor are greeted by the statue of a mermaid sitting on a rock — the same little mermaid in Hans Christian Andersen's beloved tale. Andersen, born in 1805, is Denmark's most famous author. He wrote almost two hundred fairy tales, including *The Little Mermaid*.

Little Mermaid

Mount Everest

Where in the world is it?
The Himalaya Mountains
on the border of China and Nepal

The tallest mountain in the world, Mount Everest towers 29,028 feet (8,848 meters) above sea level — almost 5½ miles (8.9 kilometers) high! On May 29, 1953, Sir Edmund Hillary of New Zealand and his Nepalese guide, Tenzing Norgay, became the first people to reach the top of Mount Everest. If you ever visit Mount Everest, watch out for the legendary Abominable Snowman!

Mount Everest

Mount Fuji

Where in the world is it?
Honshu, Japan

At 12,388 feet (3,776 meters), Mount Fuji is the highest mountain in Japan. Once it was a volcano, but it is no longer active. Just below the summit is a religious shrine, built over two thousand years ago to try to please the angry mountain. Many Japanese believe that the mountain is a holy place, and thousands of people make the long journey to the top every summer.

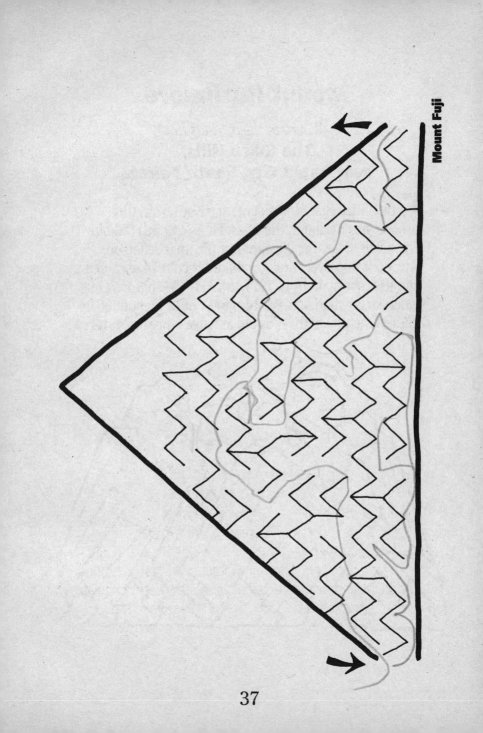

Mount Fuji

Mount Rushmore

Where in the world is it?
The Black Hills,
near Rapid City, South Dakota

Four United States presidents stare out from this famous granite cliff in the Black Hills of South Dakota. The heads of George Washington, Thomas Jefferson, Theodore Roosevelt, and Abraham Lincoln were carved into the mountain from 1927 to 1941. The figures are much larger than life: Washington's head is about 60 feet (18 meters) high — as tall as a five-story building!

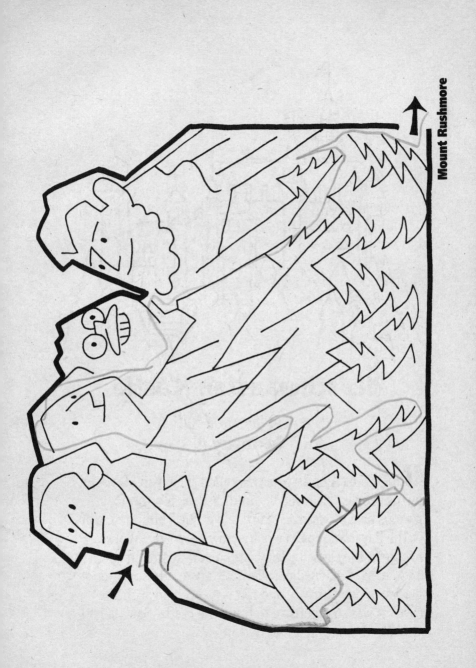

Mount Rushmore

Neuschwanstein Castle

Where in the world is it?
Germany

King Louis II of Bavaria was called "Mad King Ludwig" by his people. He loved to build castles. His most famous project was this "fairy-tale castle," built on a cliff in the Bavarian Alps in what is now Germany. Work began on the castle in 1869, and it still wasn't finished in 1886 when Ludwig died. Neuschwanstein has an indoor garden, a two-story throne room — even an artificial cave. It was so expensive to build the castle, Bavaria had almost no money left for anything else!

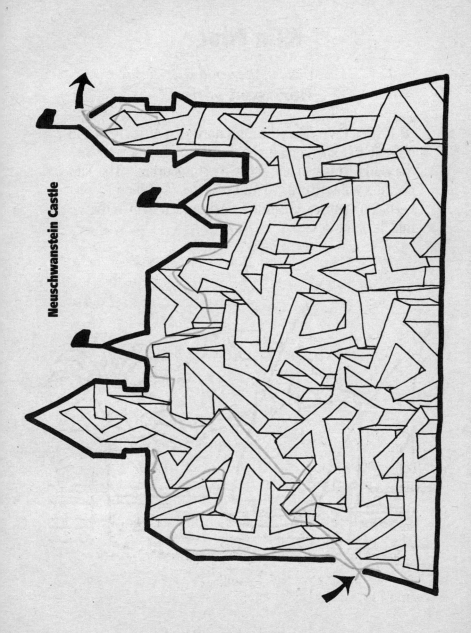

Neuschwanstein Castle

Nile River

Where in the world is it?
Northeast Africa

The Nile River flows through northeast Africa for 4,145 miles (6,671 kilometers), making it the longest river in the world. It is also one of the most important. The Nile provides water to over 10 million acres (4 million hectares) of Africa, creating a fertile green strip in the middle of the desert.

Nile River

Parthenon

Where in the world is it?
Athens, Greece

The Greeks living in Athens wanted to honor Athena, the goddess of wisdom for whom their city was named. So they built a beautiful white marble temple called the Parthenon. Built between 447 and 432 B.C., the Parthenon was originally decorated with colorful sculptures. Today you can see some of those sculptures in museums in Athens, London, and other cities. The ruins of the Parthenon still stand on a hill called the Acropolis, and many people go to see them each year.

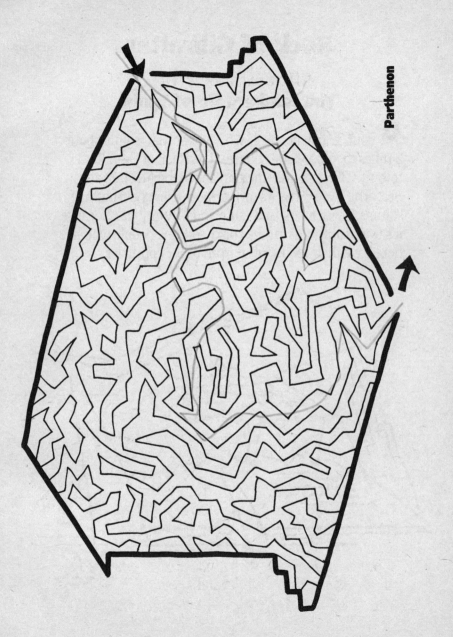

Parthenon

Rock of Gibraltar

Where in the world is it?
The southern tip of Spain

A bout 35,000 people live on a rock that is only about 2 miles (5 kilometers) square. The Rock of Gibraltar towers 1,398 feet (426 meters) above the Mediterranean Sea. The "Rock" has its own airport, currency, postage stamps, newspapers, and radio and TV stations. Because it's impossible to farm the rocky soil, the people who live here have their food sent in from other countries.

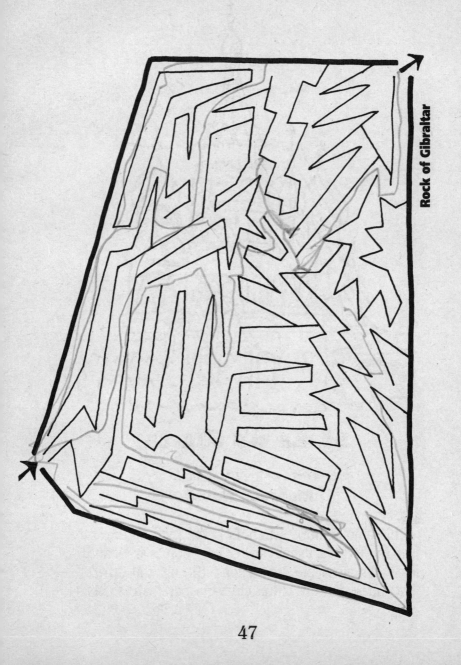

Rock of Gibraltar

47

St. Basil's Church

Where in the world is it?
Moscow, Russia

This famous church was built in the 1500s by the czar Ivan the Terrible. Its rainbow-colored domes are shaped like bulbs, pineapples, and onions. Sitting in Moscow's Red Square, it is one of this city's most dramatic sights.

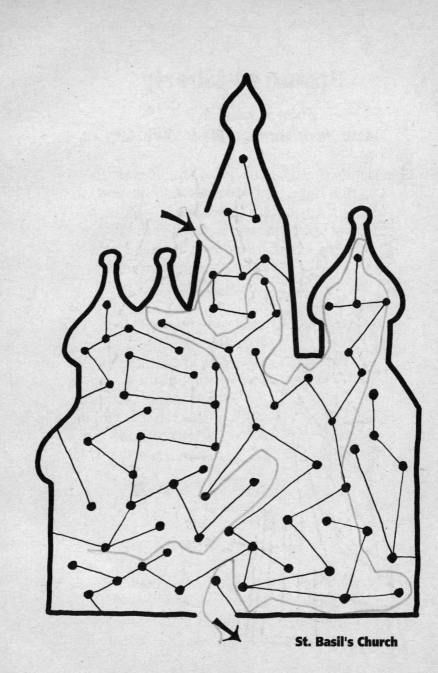

St. Basil's Church

Statue of Liberty

Where in the world is it?
New York Harbor, New York City

Standing twenty times the size of a real-life woman, this lady is the best-known statue in America. Presented to the United States by the people of France, the statue celebrates the ideals of freedom and democracy. Her right hand holds a burning torch representing the light of freedom, and her left hand holds a tablet inscribed with the date of the Declaration of Independence. You can climb all the way up into the crown, which has seven spikes for the seven continents and seven seas of the world.

Statue of Liberty

Stonehenge

Where in the world is it?
Salisbury Plain in southwest England

No one is really sure who carried the huge, heavy stones to Salisbury Plain and arranged them in such a precise pattern. It might have been Druids or some other prehistoric people. The shadows at Stonehenge move as the sun strikes the stones at different angles at different times of the year. What do the patterns mean? Some people think Stonehenge was a kind of calendar. Others think it was a place of worship. We do know that it took hundreds of years to complete the monument — and create a centuries-old mystery.

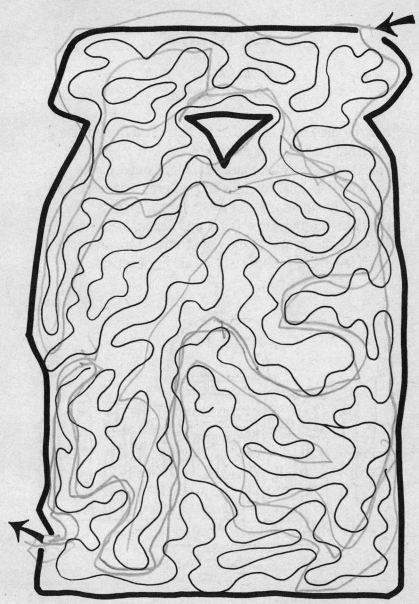

Stonehenge Stones

53

Taj Mahal

Where in the world is it?
Agra, India

An Indian ruler named Shah Jahan had this stunning tomb built for his wife, Mumtaz Mahal. It took twenty years to construct the marble building and decorate it with intricate inlaid designs and patterns of flowers made of precious stones from far away: carnelian from Baghdad, turquoise from Tibet and Persia, malachite from Russia, diamonds and onyx from central India. Shah Jahan and his beloved wife are buried inside.

Taj Mahal

U.S. Capitol

Where in the world is it?
Washington, D.C.

Congress meets in this famous office building, which is also a symbol of the United States. One branch of Congress, the Senate, meets in the north wing. The other branch, the House of Representatives, meets in the south wing. In between is a domed rotunda, or circular room. There are 540 rooms in the Capitol, which contain many paintings, sculptures, and historical items. The dome of the Capitol dazzles like white marble, but it is really made of cast iron painted a glossy white.

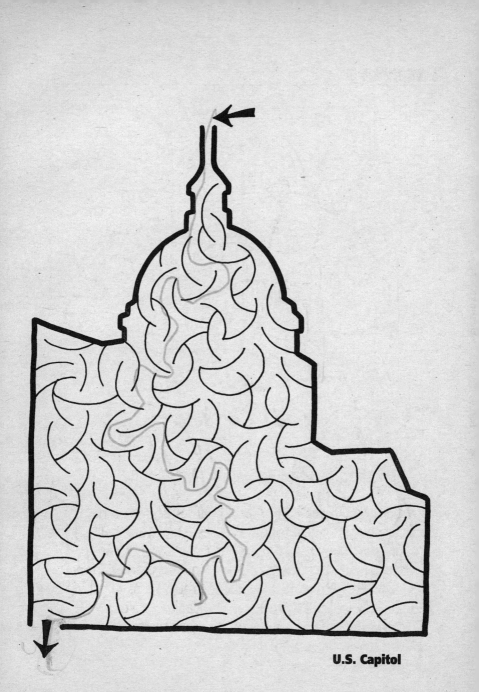

U.S. Capitol

Answers

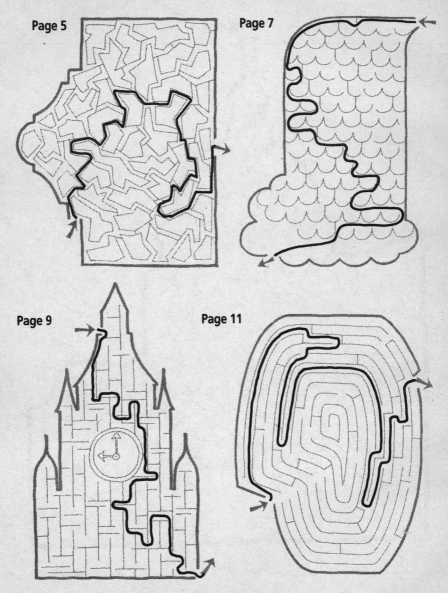

Page 5

Page 7

Page 9

Page 11

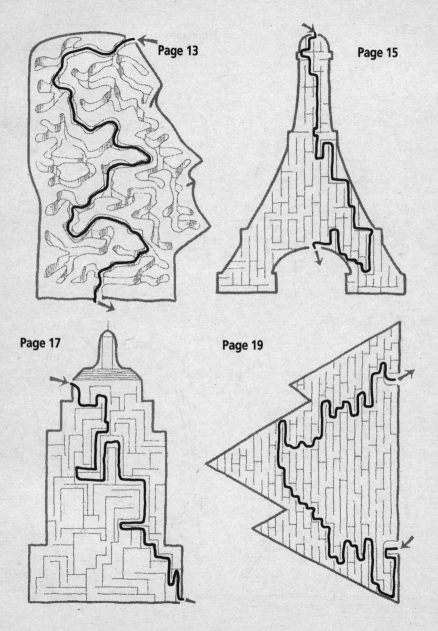

Page 13

Page 15

Page 17

Page 19

59

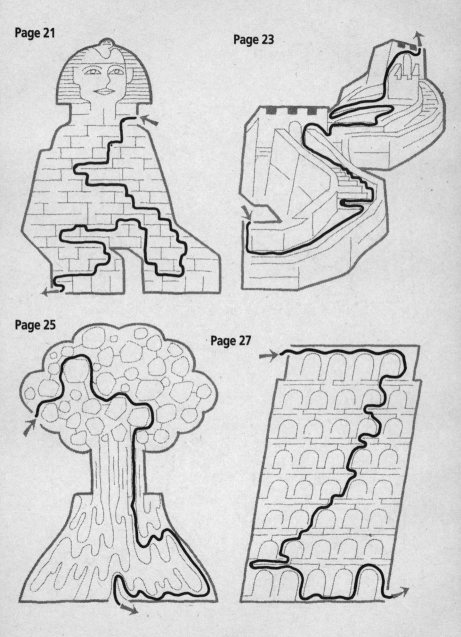

Page 21

Page 23

Page 25

Page 27

Page 29

Page 31

Page 33

Page 35

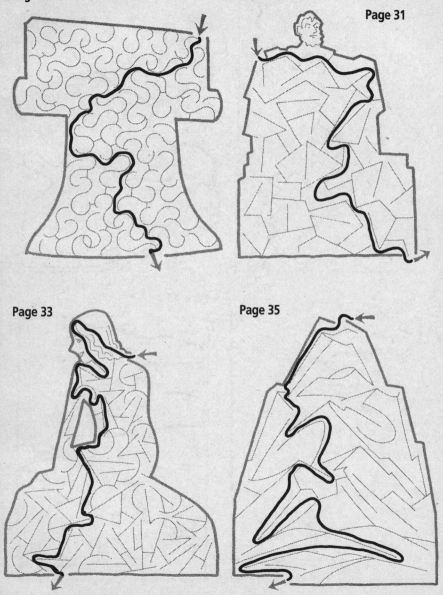

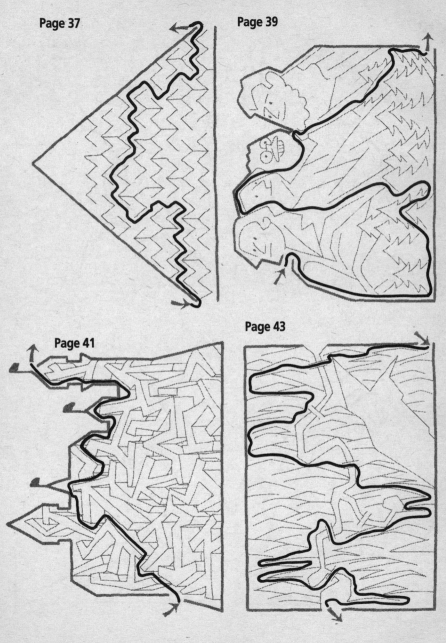

Page 37

Page 39

Page 41

Page 43

62

Page 45

Page 47

Page 49

Page 51

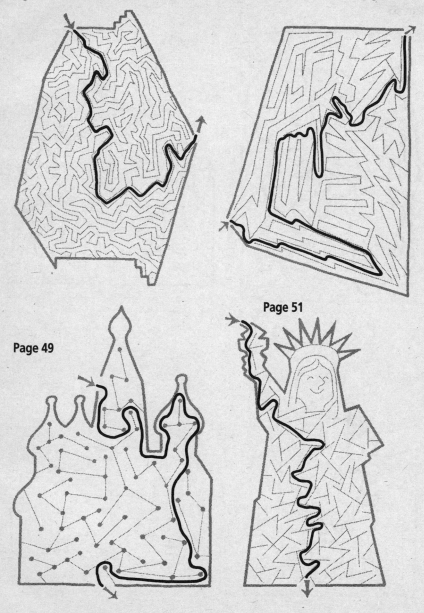

63

Page 53

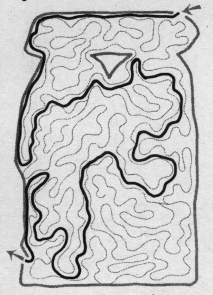

Page 55

Page 57

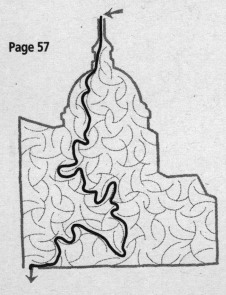